Robert Dale Owen

The Policy of Emancipation

Vol. 1

Robert Dale Owen

The Policy of Emancipation
Vol. 1

ISBN/EAN: 9783337402136

Printed in Europe, USA, Canada, Australia, Japan

Cover: Foto ©Suzi / pixelio.de

More available books at **www.hansebooks.com**

POLICY OF EMANCIPATION:

IN THREE LETTERS

THE SECRETARY OF WAR,

THE PRESIDENT OF THE UNITED STATES,

AND

THE SECRETARY OF THE TREASURY.

BY

ROBERT DALE OWEN,

LATE AMERICAN MINISTER TO NAPLES.

ADVERTISEMENT.

THE three following letters were originally published, the first and last in the "New York Evening Post," and that to the President in the "New York Daily Tribune."

They obtained, through the periodical press in all parts of the country, a wide circulation. Discussing, as they do, the great question of the day—a question on the true solution of which may depend the very life of the nation —it is believed that the public will welcome their publication in a more permanent form.

THE POLICY OF EMANCIPATION.

THE WAY OUT.

LETTER I.

TO THE SECRETARY OF WAR.

1*

LETTER TO THE SECRETARY OF WAR.

Editorial from the New York EVENING POST *of August 8, 1862.*

A STRONG WORD IN SEASON.

WE have not published, since the beginning of the war, a more significant or persuasive document than the following letter of ROBERT DALE OWEN to Secretary Stanton. The style and tone of it indicate that it was not intended for the public eye, having been sent some ten days ago to the eminent public officer to whom it is addressed—an old friend of Mr. Owen's of many years' standing—in the unreserved freedom of private correspondence; but coming by chance under the observation of several gentlemen of this city, they solicited a copy of it from Mr. Owen for publication. He cheerfully complied with the request, in the hope that his views might be useful to others.

Mr. Owen is well known in this country as a gentleman on whom the democratic party has hitherto largely bestowed its confidence; he was for many years one of its representatives in Congress from the State of Indiana, subsequently our minister at the Neapolitan court, and is now the associate of Judge Holt in the investigation and settlement of complicated transactions of the government. In all his public trusts he has discharged his duties with fidelity, ability, and honor. A careful observer of men and things, accustomed to habits of impartial thought, he has studied the phenomena of our civil war without taking much active part in events, and the results of his studies we have in this brief letter to Mr. Stanton. Mr. Owen sees, what hundreds of other democrats had begun to see before him, that there can be no speedy, satisfactory or final termination of this war until slavery is, in some way or other, put in process of extinction.

We are not authorized to speak for Mr. Stanton himself, nor for Judge Holt, nor for General Dix; but if certain rumors that have come to us are not greatly exaggerated, we think we should not be far wrong in claiming for them a general concurrence in the reasonings of Mr. Owen. Be that as it may, we know that other leading democrats, no less eminent than these, have been brought, by the experiences of the past few months, to arrive at the same conclusions. We know, for instance, that such men as Daniel S. Dickinson, Francis B. Cutting, ex-Governor Boutwell, Orestes A. Brownson, General Mitchel, General Hunter, General Lew. Wallace, General Rousseau, General Dumont, General Cochrane, and others of less note, make no concealment of their convictions that the war must put an end to slavery or slavery will put an end to the Union. These men were all democrats. Could the old conditions of political parties be restored they would, doubtless, be democrats again; but they are not democrats who refuse to be taught by events, or who, like the old Bourbons, never forget and never learn anything. They see that the outbreak of a slaveholders' war has changed essentially the relations of slavery to the State, and they guide their minds, not by the old party traditions, or according to circumstances which have forever passed away, but by the light of existing events.

We of the North can no doubt whip the rebels by arms; we can drive them out of Richmond into the cotton States; we can pursue them through the thousand swamps of the cotton States into the Gulf of Mexico; it would take time and money and life to do so; but we could do it all beyond a peradventure. But the Union would not be thereby restored. The same elements of discord would still exist; the same feuds would break out; and no permanent peace or permanent harmony would be possible until the respective social systems of the North and South are rendered homogeneous by the extinction of the only difference between them. We must go on fighting forever in this kind of desultory civil war; or else we must form coterminous states of diverse civilizations, which would fight no less perpetually ; or finally, looking the problem right in the heart of it, resolve to restore the Union on the only basis on which, after what has occurred, a restoration seems to be possible, namely, the establishment of free institutions and a free system of society in all the component parts.

THE WAY OUT.

TO THE HON. EDWIN M. STANTON,
SECRETARY OF WAR.

MY political antecedents are known to you. Always a democrat, but never a pro-slavery democrat ; opposed, in principle and feeling, from my youth up, to human slavery, but believing, until recently, that, in the interests of liberty itself, it was the part of wisdom in the North to abstain from interference with the danger-fraught domestic institution of the South, and to trust to time for its eradication ; opposed, with a hereditary aversion, to war, I was willing, before the sword was drawn, to make any honorable concessions that might avert its horrors.

But political convulsions bring with them great lessons and new duties. War would not, under the Divine economy, have been permitted, as in all past ages it has been, if it had not its mission. But to attain the good it brings we must recognize its necessities.

No civil war of proportions so gigantic as that now raging ever existed in the world before. It differs from all others, both in the results sure to ensue from its protraction beyond a brief period, and in the conditions under which, out of evil, it may eventuate in good. In calculating these, time is an essential element.

Seven or eight hundred millions are spent. At the best, as much more is likely to go. Two thousand millions or upward is not an improbable total. That is half the national debt of England; and the interest on it (probably at almost double the rate she pays) will make our annual burden nearly equal to hers. If the war lasts three years longer, these figures may be doubled. It must not last three years longer, unless we are willing to risk national bankruptcy.

How is it to be terminated?

By concession? That is no longer in our power. We can buy a truce, a pause, by concession to the South; nothing more.

By force of arms then? But if by force, it must be quickly done. Delay is defeat.

And it must be effectually done. After one such war the nation may revive, its energies still elastic; solvent still, and respected. A second will ruin it financially, to say nothing of worse ruin. To save the country, then, the war must not terminate without a sufficient guaranty against its resumption.

How can the war be quickly and effectually terminated? What guaranty is sufficient that it will not be resumed?

Gradually, very gradually, as this contest proceeded, have I been approaching the conviction that there is but one such guaranty: the emancipation of negro slaves throughout this continent. Perhaps—but as to this I am less certain—that measure is the only sure means of terminating, quickly and effectually, this war. The recent reverse under General McClellan, the scattered rebel fires daily bursting forth in States which our forces had already overrun, the fact that we are fighting against brave men of our own race, all increase the probability that we must deprive the South of a legal right to its four millions of laborers, before we can succeed against their masters in a reasonable time and in an effectual manner.

I am not an advocate of revolutionary short-cuts out of a difficulty. I am not in favor of violating the Constitution by way of escaping a danger. There might be immediate advantage, but the precedent is replete with peril.

Could slavery have been abolished, by northern action, while peace yet existed between the North and South, without a violation of the Constitution? in other words, without a revolutionary act? Clearly not. Can slavery be eradicated now, in war, without such violation? If emancipation be necessary to insure the permanent peace and safety of our government, and if we are willing to pay to all loyal slave-owners a reasonable price for their slaves, clearly yes.

For no principle in law is better established than this, that when important public interests demand it, private property may be taken, at a fair appraisement, for public use. The opening of a street in improving a city, the running of a railroad, are held, in this and other civilized countries, to be objects of sufficient importance to justify what the French law calls *"appropriation forcée pour cause d'utilité publique."*

But of importance how utterly trivial is the opening of a street or of a railroad compared to the preservation, in its integrity, of the greatest republic upon earth!

Ought we to declare general emancipation, coupled with a provision for the payment, to all loyal slave-holders, of the fairly appraised value of their slaves? This question resolves itself into another: Have things gone so far that the Union, in its peaceful integrity, and negro slavery within its borders, can no longer co-exist? That is THE GREAT QUESTION OF THE DAY. I think it must be answered, even now, in the affirmative. Every month that passes is converting hundreds of thousands of moderate and conservative and peace-loving men to the same opinion. They despair of sectional friendship or national peace, until the teeming cause of mortal hatred and civil war is rooted out forever.

Have we the means of paying loyal slave-owners a fair price for their slaves? If we act now, before a protracted contest has exhausted our resources, yes. If we wait the termination of a three or four years' war, very certainly, no.

In that price deportation must not be estimated. The South asserts that negro slaves are indispensable to her. That is only so far true, that she does absolutely need hired negro workmen, and ought not to be deprived of them. Her agriculture would, for a time, be ruined without them. But no good man desires a settlement under which any section of our country would be even temporarily ruined.

Nor can it be doubted that the South, however strong

2

her prejudices and traditions in favor of owning her laborers, has herself been brought, by the perils of the hour, to
think seriously of a change of system as the only means
left her to obtain aid and comfort from Europe. Nor can
all her leaders be wholly blind to the fact that such a
change of system would advance, in the end, beyond calculation, her material prosperity.

Suppose a declaration, to the effect that the government,
urged by the necessity of self-preservation, takes, at a fair val-
uation, the slave property of the South. Will such a declaration cause a negro insurrection and indiscriminate assassina-
tion of whites throughout the slave States? The result, so
far, has clearly shown that the negro, mild and long-suffering,
and often attached to his owner, is little disposed to resist,
under an organization of his own. Once assured of freedom, he will gradually join our cause—that is all. He can
then be hired as laborer or soldier, as may seem fit—payment being made for him if his master proves to be loyal,
and his services being confiscated if these are due to a rebel.
In all this we are clearly in our right.

Look now at the question in its foreign aspect, under the
chances of European intervention. Be those chances great
or small, intervention may occur, and that ere long.

If it occur, its character will chiefly depend upon what
shall have been the antecedent action of our government in
regard to slavery.

If, previously to such intervention, we shall have issued
a general declaration of emancipation, then we shall stand
before Europe as the champions of human liberty, while

our enemies will be regarded as the advocates of human servitude. Public opinion in England, in France, and throughout Europe generally, will then prevent the respective governments from intervening, except it be in our favor. No European government dare place itself in the attitude of a slavery protector.

If, on the contrary, we shall have left the issue as it now stands, our policy indicated only by the Confiscation act, not broadly and boldly announced, and more especially if the South, despairing of saving her favorite institution, concedes, as the price of foreign recognition and support, a voluntary system of gradual emancipation—not at all an unlikely move—then the sympathy of public opinion throughout Europe will be with the South, and will sustain any action in her favor.

Think too, in such an event, how false our position! how low we shall have fallen in the eyes of the world! how unenviable the place we shall occupy in history through all time!

It is idle gasconade to say, that thus situated, we can defy Europe. Let the South, by conceding emancipation, secure the sympathy and the permanent services of her four millions of laborers, without action of ours; then throw into the scale against us the thirty millions of England, the forty millions of France—and who shall say how many tens of millions besides?—and what chance for success or for reputation shall we have, struggling for nothing nobler than self-existence, in equivocal attitude before the world, matched against opponents who shall have forestalled us and assumed the initiative of progress?

While the contest assumes no higher character than that of a portion of a great nation desiring a separation from the mother country and forcibly casting off its authority, what more sympathy can we expect from Europe than we ourselves gave to Spain when she lost Mexico, or to Mexico when Texas struck for independence? Until the issue is changed, so that the great question of human liberty becomes involved in it, we must expect from European powers at the best only indifference; coupled, probably, with the feeling, that as Mexico succeeded against Spain, and Texas against Mexico, so will a Southern Confederacy finally maintain itself against us.

That a declaration of emancipation was not issued a year ago, I do not regret. Great changes must mature in public opinion before they can be safely carried out. Extreme measures, to be justified and to be effectual, must often be preceded by long-tried conciliation. Yet in national emergencies it may be as dangerous to disappoint as to anticipate public opinion. And I confess my fears for the result if decisive measures are longer delayed.

Stand where we are we cannot; and to go on is less dangerous than to retrace our steps. We ought never to have proposed emancipation with compensation to loyal slave-owners, nor declared to the disloyal, as by law we have, that their slaves shall be liberated without compensation, if we did not intend to follow out the policy we commenced. We have incurred the odium; let us reap the benefit.

Nor do I perceive how we can free the slaves of rebels, yet reasonably expect to retain slavery in the border States, even in case they persist in refusing the offer of the President. Having intervened so far, extirpation of slavery, the only effectual policy, becomes the safest also.

All men in the North will not acquiesce. Neither did all acquiesce when the war was commenced; yet who that is loyal opposes it now? And what would have been the result had we waited, ere we commenced the war, for unanimity?

Some will fall off. So be it. There is small loss in that. And there is some gain. Better an open enemy than a worthless friend. It is time that men were taking sides. As things now stand I see no use in conciliating the half-loyal. He who is not for us is against us.

I think the people are ready. I believe that the loyal citizens of the North, with such small proportion of exceptions as in radical national changes must be disregarded, are to-day prepared for emancipation. They have paid for it in treasure, in blood; not by their option. They feel that the sacrifices they have made, and have still to make, are too vast to have been incurred, except in purchase of a great pledge of perpetual safety and peace.

Reflecting men feel, too, that such a pledge is a national, not merely a northern, necessity. The South, exhausted and suffering, needs it to the full as much as we. She will soon perceive, if she does not already, that two parts of one nation, or even two coterminous nations, can never again exist in amity on this continent, one slave and the other free. She cannot but see that fugitive-slave law difficulties, if no others existed, would suffice to prevent this.

It is not the question whether a paper declaration, easily

issued, will or will not be followed by a thousand practical difficulties. The uprooting of an ancient and gigantic abuse always involves such. Nor should we be called upon to predict in advance (for who can entirely foresee?) how each of these will be ultimately solved. The true question is, whether greater difficulties, even insuperable ones, do not beset any other policy. Pressed home as we are, to avoid obstacles is impossible. We can but select the least formidable. The lives of the best of us are spent in choosing between evils.

When dangers surround us we must walk, in a measure, by faith. Let us do what we can, and leave to God the issue. We may best trust to Him when we enter His path of progress. He aids those who walk in it.

I feel assured that final success awaits us in pursuing such a path, and I see no other road out of the darkness.

ROBERT DALE OWEN.

NEW YORK, July 23, 1862.

THE TWENTY-THIRD OF SEPTEMBER.

LETTER II.

TO THE PRESIDENT.

LETTER TO THE PRESIDENT.

———— ——

Editorial from the New York DAILY TRIBUNE *of October* 23, 1862.

WE publish this morning—by express permission obtained at Washington—a letter from ROBERT DALE OWEN, of Indiana, to the President of the United States. This eloquent and forcible appeal for a Proclamation of Emancipation as a war measure—sure to meet with the approbation of all loyal men, and to carry confusion into the camp of the enemy—was received by the President a few days before the Proclamation was issued. Precisely what influence it may have exercised on the author of that Proclamation we do not know, but we do know, from private sources as well as from the frequent allusions that have been made to it by the correspondents of public journals in Washington, that it was regarded by others of high official position as a succinct and admirable statement of the whole question. Regarding it as a valuable illustration of the history of the times, and all the more so that it comes from one who has long been a distinguished member of the democratic party, we gladly avail ourselves of the permission to publish it.   Though a month only has elapsed since it was written, events are already justifying the foresight that dictated it.

THE TWENTY-THIRD OF SEPTEMBER.

TO THE PRESIDENT
OF THE UNITED STATES.

In days when the public safety is imminently threatened, and the fate of a nation may hang upon a single act, we owe frank speech, above all other men, to him who is highest in authority.   I shall speak to you as man to man.

Harsh opinions have been formed of you; even honest men doubting the probity of your intentions.   I do not share their doubts.   I believe you to be upright, single-hearted in your desire to rescue the country in the hour of her utmost need without after-thought of the personal consequences to yourself.

If, amid the multitude of contending counsel, you have hesitated and doubted; if, when a great measure suggested itself, you have shrunk from the vast responsibility, afraid to go forward lest you should go wrong, what wonder? How few, since the foundation of the world, have found themselves in a position environed with public perils so numerous, oppressed with responsibilities so high and solemn, as yourself!

No man ever escaped from such—so reads the lesson of history—without a bold heart and a high faith.   Wisdom,

prudence, forethought, these are essential. But not second
to these is that noble courage which adventures the right,
and leaves the consequences to God.

Men ever follow willingly a daring leader: most willingly
of all, in great emergencies. Boldness and decision com-
mand, often even in evil, the respect and concurrence of
mankind. How much more in good!

There is a measure needing courage to adopt and enforce it, which I believe to be of virtue sufficient to redeem
the nation in this its darkest hour: one only; I know of no
other to which we may rationally trust for relief from im-
pending dangers without and within.

The dangers which threaten us are twofold: First, from
the Confederate forces, composed of men whose earnest
convictions and reckless bravery it is idle to deny. Secondly,
from ourselves, compelled to make use of a military power
of proportions so gigantic that no nation ever permitted
the existence of such without more or less risk to the people
who employed it. If we think lightly of this latter danger,
we slight the teachings of all past time.

As to the first: Have you not had your moments of
doubt whether we are to succeed at all?—whether the
Union, once so glorious, will ever be reunited?—whether
peace, which we used to enjoy with as little gratitude
as we do the sunlight or the air we breathe, will ever again
settle down over our distracted country?

If I have doubts of all this, it is only because I do not
know what your action will be. We have at our disposal
the means of certain success; but I cannot tell whether,
while there is yet time, you will decide to employ them.

Our enemies, like the Grecian hero, have one vulnerable point. You have not touched it yet. What should have been their element of weakness has been suffered to remain an element of strength.

They have nearly a million of able-bodied men of fit age for war or for labor. Holding these men in bondage, and employing them to till the soil, they are enabled to send to the battle-field almost their entire white male adult population, yet preserve their commissariat sufficiently supplied.

It has always been a great wrong that these men and their families should be held in bondage. We of the North have hitherto acquiesced in it, lest, in the endeavor to redress it in violation of the Constitution, greater evils might ensue.

But the time has come when it *is* constitutional to redress it. The rebellion has made it so. Property in man, always morally unjust, has become nationally dangerous. Property that endangers the safety of a nation should not be suffered to remain in the hands of its citizens. A chief magistrate who permits it so to remain becomes responsible for the consequences. For he has the right, under the law and the Constitution, to take private property, with just compensation offered, for public use, whenever it is apparent that any public exigency demands such appropriation.

Forgive what may seem curt speech if I say that, in my judgment, a President with a just sense of duty has no option in such a case.

In the due exercise of your official power, in strictest accordance with law and the Constitution, you can deprive the enemy of that which, above all else, has given, and still gives him, aid and comfort. You can declare emancipated his slaves, the suppliers of his commissariat. Gradually, you can deprive him of these; and for every hundred thousand productive laborers he loses, you may have a hundred thousand soldiers. With their aid you can reach the rest. What then remains for him? He must thin his ranks to cultivate his plantations. He must labor for his own food, or must perish for the lack of it.

The people are forbidden to give aid and comfort to rebels. What of a government that has the power to cut off from aid and comfort all the rebels of the South and fails to exercise it?

We ought to do that which is right, even if the recompense be distant and uncertain; but we add folly to injustice if we neglect a great act of beneficence that is to be rewarded, even now, by our own preservation.

Yet again. Can you look forward to the future of our country and imagine any state of things in which, with slavery still existing, we should be assured of permanent peace? I cannot. We can constitutionally extirpate slavery at this time. But if we fail to do this, then, unless we intend hereafter to violate the Constitution, we shall have a fugitive slave law in operation whenever the war is over. Shall the North have sacrificed a hundred thousand lives and two thousand millions of treasure to come to that at last? Not even a guaranty of peace purchased at so enormous a cost? After voluntary exertions on the part of our people to which the history of the world furnishes no parallel, is the old root of bitterness still to re-

3

main in the ground, to sprout and bear fruit in the future
as it has borne fruit in the past?

The questions are addressed to you. For upon you and
upon your action more than upon any other one thing does
the answer depend. You have, at this time, more power
than any constitutional monarch in the world. The English
government always acts according to the policy approved
by the constitutional advisers of the Crown. You would
violate usage only if you should act without the advice, or
even contrary to the opinions, of your constitutional advisers. I do not mean that you could continue to do this
with propriety or even with safety; I merely assert that
the power is, in point of fact, in your hands. And for such
a power, what a responsibility to God and man!

It is within your power at this very moment not only to
consummate an act of enlightened statesmanship, but, as
the instrument of the Almighty, to restore to freedom a
race of men. If you are tempted by an imperishable
name it is within your reach. We may look through
ancient and modern history, yet scarce find a sovereign to
whom God offered the privilege of bestowing on humanity
a boon so vast.

Such an offer comes to no human being twice. It is
made to you to-day. How long it will remain open—
whether in three months or in one month from now it will
still be at your option to accept it—God, who reads the
hearts of men, alone knows.

And this brings me to speak of another class of dangers
—those which may arise here in the North, among ourselves.

Do you read the daily newspaper press, that wonderful and instructive modern index of the passing opinions of the times? If so, have you not recently seen there signs that startled you?—advice, audaciously given in certain quarters, that it is time the army should take the power into its own hands and demand the dismissal from your cabinet of the best men in it? Have you no facts in your own experience going to prove that such audacity has not shown its head without power and numbers that render it formidable? I do not fear it; not now, if it is strangled at its birth. But he tempts Providence who suffers that spirit of anarchy to grow and gather strength before striking a blow for its destruction.

You cannot be ignorant of the design of these men. He that runs may read it. They see that we are drifting toward emancipation. They see that the demand from the masses of our people for this great measure is becoming, day by day, more importunate. They know that a majority of your cabinet favor it. They feel assured, as to yourself, that if the option remain with you, it is but a question of time and of form when and how a proclamation of emancipation will be issued. They perceive but one power that has any chance successfully to arrest this stream and coerce your action. Openly they appeal to it. Openly they declare that cabinet ministers must be imposed upon you by military dictation. No other course is left them to effect their great object, namely, to perpetuate among us that slavery which the nation, with a determination which increases from day to day, is resolved to uproot.

One blow may be dealt by you against these men that

will crush forever their treasonable cabals. It is the same that lays the foundation of peace, and assures, beyond possible peradventure, the downfall of the rebellion. They know their danger. They read EMANCIPATION in all the signs of the times. It is to them the handwriting on the wall, foreshadowing their political fate. What wonder that they resort to desperate means to arrest its advent?

Shall they be allowed time, by insidious argument, to entice the unwary into the ranks of sedition? By prompt action alone can you prevent it. It is idle to await unanimity. Men acquiesce in a thousand things, once righteously and boldly done, to which, if proposed to them in advance, they might find endless objections.

Do you hesitate? Will you delay the blow? See to it, that when at last your resolution is taken, the power may not already have passed away from your hands.

The twenty-third of September approaches—the date when the sixty-day notice you have given to the rebels will expire—expire without other reply to your warning than the invasion of Maryland and a menace to Pennsylvania. Is it to rest there? Patiently we have waited the time. Is nothing to follow? Are our enemies to boast that we speak brave words—and there an end of it?

What a day, if you but will it, may that twenty-third of September become! The very turning point in the nation's fate! A day to the rebels of despair, to every loyal heart of exultant rejoicing! A day of which the anniversary will be celebrated with jubilee while the American Union endures! A day to be remembered not in our land alone, but wherever humanity mourns over the wrongs of the slave, or rejoices in his liberation!

You are the first President to whom the opportunity was ever offered constitutionally to inaugurate such a day. If you fail us now, you may be the last. Lift then the weight from the heart of this people. Let them breathe free once more. Extirpate the blighting curse, a living threat throughout long years past, that has smitten at last with desolation a land to which God had granted everything but wisdom and justice. Give back to the nation its hope and faith in a future of peace and undisturbed prosperity. Fulfill—you can far more than fulfill—the brightest anticipations of those who, in the name of human freedom, and in the face of threats that have ripened into terrible realities since, fought that battle which placed you where you now stand.

ROBERT DALE OWEN.

New York, Sept. 17, 1862.

[This letter was placed in the hands of the President on Friday, September 19.]

3*

CONDITIONS OF LASTING PEACE.

LETTER III.

TO THE SECRETARY OF THE TREASURY.

LETTER TO THE SECRETARY OF THE TREASURY.

Editorial from the New York EVENING POST *of November 22, 1862.*

THE COST OF PEACE.

WE publish elsewhere a discussion of the aspects and duties of the times, by one of our most distinguished statesmen and politicians, ROBERT DALE OWEN. Unlike some other democrats Mr. Owen does not deceive himself as to the nature of the civil war in which we are engaged. He takes no narrow or partisan view of the motives under which it should be conducted. He desires no end of it which shall not be enduring in its results.

MR. Owen discerns what many had long since discerned before, and many more are just beginning to discern, that the continued existence of two orders of society, so different as those of the free and slave States, is incompatible with the peace of the continent. Whether in the Union or out of it, slavery can only prove a cause of perpetual irritation and conflict, and a suspension of hostilities or truce of any kind a mere postponement of a more dreadful outbreak. Emancipation is at once the surest means of suppressing the rebellion as an armed resistance, and of harmonizing the sections as bodies politic.

His statements are clear, his arguments cogent, his motives patriotic, and we ask for his presentation of the case the calm, unprejudiced consideration of men of all parties, and particularly of that democratic party to which the writer has all his life adhered.

CONDITIONS OF LASTING PEACE.

TO THE HON. SALMON P. CHASE,
SECRETARY OF THE TREASURY.

SIR : In briefest terms I state the propositions which, as the subject of our recent conversation, I promised to reduce to writing.

What are the reasonable hopes of peace?

Not, that within the next fifty days the South, availing herself of the term of grace offered in the President's proclamation, may, to save her favorite institution, return to her allegiance. Let us not deceive ourselves. There are *no* conditions, *no* guarantees — no, not if we proffer a blank-sheet on which to set them down, with unrestricted pen, in her own hand—under which she will consent to reunion, except in one contingency—conquest, more or less complete, by force of arms.

Are we likely to obtain peace by conquest?

In search of an answer, let us look closely at a few statistical facts.

By the census of 1860, the number of white males between the ages of 18 and 45 is, in the loyal States, about four millions; and in the disloyal States, about one million

three hundred thousand; a little upwards of three to one
The disproportion seems overwhelmingly great.

But this calculation, as a basis of military strength, is
wholly fallacious; for it includes persons of one color only.

Out of the above four millions the North has to provide
soldiers and (with inconsiderable exceptions, not usually
extending to field labor) laborers also.

But of the three millions and a half of slaves owned in
the rebel States, about two millions may be estimated as
laborers   Allow three hundred thousand of these as employed in domestic services and other occupations followed
by women among us, and we have seventeen hundred thousand plantation hands, male and female, each one of which
counts against a northern laborer on farm or in work-shop.

Then, of that portion of population whence soldiers and
out-door laborers and mechanics must chiefly be taken, the
Northern States have four millions and the Southern States
three millions

Supposing the negroes all loyal to their masters, it fol-
lows that the true proportion of strength available in this
war—that is, of soldiers to fight and laborers to support
the nation while fighting—may fairly enough be taken at
three in the South to four in the North.

Under this supposition of a South united, without regard
to color in an effort for recognition, shall we obtain peace
by subduing her?   If history teach truth, we shall not.
Never, since the world began, did nine millions of people
band together, resolutely inspired by the one idea of achiev-
ing their independence, yet fail to obtain it   It is not a century since one-third of the number successfully defied Great
Britain

But let us suppose the negroes of the South loyal to the Union instead of to their masters, how stands the matter then?

In that case, it is not to a united people, but to a confederacy divided against itself, that we are opposed; the masters on one side; the laborers, exceeding them in number, on the other.

Suppose the services of these laborers transferred to us, what will then be the proportion, on either side, of forces available, directly and indirectly, for military purposes?

As about five and three-fourths to one and a third: in other words, nearly *as nine to two.*

Such a wholesale transfer is, of course, impossible in practice. But in so far as the transfer is possible, and shall occur, we approach the above results.

How much wisdom, under these circumstances, is there in the advice that we should put down the rebellion first and settle the negro question afterward? What shall we say of their statesmanship, who, in a war like this, would leave out of view the practical effects of emancipation?

On the other hand, however, it is to be admitted that African loyalty in this war will little avail us, if we have not good sense and good feeling enough properly to govern the negroes who may enter our lines.

To render their aid available: in the first place we must treat them humanely, a duty we have yet to learn; and secondly, both for their sakes and for our own, we must not support them in idleness. Doubtless, they are most efficient as laborers, as domestics in camp, as teamsters, or employed on intrenchments and fortifications, or in ambulance corps, or as sappers and miners; or, as fast as southern plantations shall fall into our possession, as field-hands. But if all these posts become over-filled, better do away with the necessity for further draft in the North by putting muskets in the hands of able-bodied men, colored differently from ourselves, than to delude their ignorance into the opinion that among the privileges of freedom is food without work.

Have we philanthropy and discretion enough wisely to administer such a change of system? Possibly not. Administrative capacity in public affairs is not our strong point. We would do well to bear in mind, however, that without such capacity not this war only, but our entire governmental experiment, will prove a failure at last.

Do other objections hold against the plan? Does humanity forbid us to accept the aid of an enslaved race? In so far as humanity can ever enjoin war at all, she *enjoins* the employment, by us of the African in this: first, because his employment may shorten, by years, the fratricidal struggle; and then, because, if he is not permitted to assist in civilized warfare under us, and if, without his aid, we fail to effect his liberation and thus disappoint his hopes, he may be overtaken by the temptation to seek freedom and revenge in his own wild way. In accepting the liberated slave as a soldier we may prevent his rising as an assassin. By the creation of negro brigades we may avert the indiscriminate massacres of servile insurrection.

Or is there an insuperable difficulty of caste in the way? In a contest likely to eventuate in securing to another race than ours the greatest of temporal blessings, are we determined to shut out that race from all share in its own liber-

4

ation? Are we so enamored of the Moloch, War, that we will suffer none but *our* sons to pass through the fire? Terrible penalty to pay, with life and death at stake, for a national prejudice against the Southern Pariah!

As to the duty of our rulers in the premises, I cannot see according to what principle of ethics a government, charged with the lives of millions, the putting down of a gigantic rebellion, and the restoring of tranquillity to the land, has the right, in the hour of its utmost need, to scorn a vast element of strength placed within its reach and at its disposal; nor why, if it refuses to avail itself of such an element, it should not be held responsible for the lives it sacrifices and the hopes it blights.

But we need emancipation far less for the material aid it affords—great, even indispensable, though it be—than because of other paramount considerations.

We have tried the experiment of a federal Union, with a free-labor system in one portion of it and a slave system in another, for eighty years; and no one familiar with our affairs for a quarter of a century past is ignorant that the result has been an increase—embittered year by year in ever-accelerated ratio—of dissensions, of sectional jealousies, of national heart-burnings. When, eighteen months since, these culminated in war, it was but the issue which our ablest statesmen, looking sorrowfully into the future, had long since foretold. But if, while yet at peace and with all the influence of revolutionary reminiscences pleading the cause of Union, this diversity of labor systems, producing variance of character and alienation of feeling, proved stronger to divide than all past memories and present interests to unite, what chance is there that its baneful power for evil should cease, now, when to thoughts of fancied injuries in other years are added the recollections of the terrible realities enacted on a hundred bloody battle-fields from which the smoke has scarcely passed away?

None—the remotest!

A suspension of hostilities we can purchase; a few years' respite, probably, in which to return to our money-getting, before the storm bursts forth anew with gathered force; but if we look beyond selfishness and the present; if our children are in our thoughts; if we are suffering and expending now, that they in a land of prosperity, may live and die in peace, then must we act so that the result shall endure. We must not be content to put off the evil day. The root of the evil—the pregnant cause of the war —that must be eradicated.

Report has it that a western politician recently proposed, as the best solution of our difficulties, the recognition of slavery in all the States. Such an idea has a basis of truth; namely, that a state of war is, among us, the necessary result of conflicting labor systems. Such an idea might even be carried out and lead to peace, but for that progressive spirit of Christian civilization which we dare not openly outrage, how imperfectly soever we obey its humane behests.

There are a thousand reasons—geographical, commercial, political, international—why we should not consent to a separation into two confederacies; it is a contingency not to be thought of or entertained; but *if we look merely to the conditions of lasting peace*, the chance of

maintaining it would be far better if the independence of
the South were to be recognized with her negroes emancipated, than if she were to return to her allegiance, re-
taining her slave system.

For in the former case, the cause of dissension being
uprooted, the tendency would be to reunite, and a few
years might see us a single nation again; while, in the
latter, a constantly active source of irritation still existing,
three years of breathing time would not elapse without
bringing endless quarrels and a second rebellion.

Conceive reunion, with slavery still in existence. Imagine
southern sympathizers in power among us offering com-
promises. Suppose the South, exhausted with military
reverses and desiring a few years' armistice to recruit,
decides to accept it under the guise of peace and recon-
struction? What next? Thousands of slaves, their excited hopes of emancipation crushed, fleeing across the
border. A fugitive slave law, revived by peace, demand-
ing their rendition. Popular opinion in the North opposed
to the law, and refusing the demand. Renewed war the
certain consequence.

Or take even the alternative of recognition—recognition
of an independent confederacy, still slave-holding. Are
we, then—becoming the sole exception among the nations
of the earth—to make ourselves aiders and abettors of the
slave system of a foreign nation, by agreeing to return to
her negro refugees seeking liberty and an asylum among
us? National self-respect imperatively forbids this. Public sentiment would compel the rejection, as a base humi-
liation, of any proposed treaty stipulation, providing for

rendition of runaway slaves. Yet the South would regard such rejection in no other light than as a standing menace—a threat to deprive her of what she regards as her most valuable property. Coterminous as for hundreds —possibly thousands—of miles our boundaries would be, must not the South, in common prudence, maintain all along that endless border line an armed slave police? Are we to consent to this? And if we do shall we escape border raids after fleeing fugitives? No sane man will expect it. Are we to suffer these? We are disgraced. Are we to resent them? It is a renewal of hostilities.

State elections may go as they will. Their results can never change the fact that any party obtaining the control of the government and adopting the policy that the settlement of the emancipation question is to be postponed till the war shall be closed will never, while it pursues that policy, see this war permanently closed—not even by accepting a shameful disruption of our country.

But if emancipation is to avail us as a peace measure, we must adopt it boldly, resolutely, effectually. It must be general not partial; extending not to the slaves of rebels only, but to every slave on this continent. Even if it were practicable, which it is not, with slavery non-existent in the Northern States and abolished in those which persist in rebellion, to maintain it in the narrow border strip, it is precisely there where negro fugitives can the most readily escape, that its maintenance would the most certainly lead to war.

Can this great peace measure be constitutionally enacted?

A proclamation or (the more appropriate form) an act of General Emancipation, should, in its preamble, set forth in substance, that the claims to service or labor of which it deprives certain persons having been proved by recent events to be of a character endangering the supremacy of the law, jeopardizing the integrity of the Union, and incompatible with the permanent peace of the country, are taken by the government, with just compensation made. Under circumstances far less urgent than these, the law or custom of civilized nations, based on considerations of public utility, authorizes such taking of private property for public use. We ourselves are familiar with its operation. When a conflagration in a city threatens to spread far, houses in the line of its progress may legally be seized and destroyed by the authorities in order to arrest it; and the owners are not held to have been wronged if they are paid for such losses under an equitable appraisement. But it is not the existence of part of a city that is now endangered; it is the integrity of one among the first powers of the world that is menaced with destruction.

The truth of the preamble suggested has become, in my judgment, incontrovertible. It will receive the assent of an overwhelming majority of the people of the loyal States. The public sentiment of Europe will admit its truth.

Let us confess that such a preamble, as preface to act or proclamation, could not have commanded the assent of more than a small fraction of our people, only two short years ago—two years, as we reckon time; a generation, if we calculate by the stirring events and far-reaching upheavals that have been crowded into the eventful months. In such days as these abuses ripen rapidly. Their consequences mature. Their ultimate tendencies become apparent. We are reminded of their transitory character. We are reminded that although for the time, and in a certain stage of human progress, some abuses may have their temporary use, and for this, under God's economy, may have been suffered to continue; yet all abuses have but a limited life. The right only is eternal.

The rebellion, teacher and creator as well as scourge and destroyer, by sternly laying bare the imminent dangers of slavery, has created the constitutionality of emancipation. It has done more. It has made emancipation a bounden political duty, as well as a strictly constitutional right.

Can we, in declaring emancipation, legally avoid the payment, say of two hundred millions, in the shape of compensation to loyal slave-holders?

Not if a slave-holder's right to service and labor from his slaves, when not forfeited by treason, is legal. On humanitarian grounds the legality of that right has been denied. But a construction of the Constitution adverse to such denial, and acquiesced in by the nation throughout more than two generations, is held by most men to be reason sufficient why the right in question should be regarded as private property. If it be private property, then, except by violating the fifth article of the amendments to the Constitution, it cannot be taken for public use without just compensation. To violate any article of the Constitution is a revolutionary act; but such acts cost a nation more than a few hundred millions of dollars.

The risk that a future decision of the Supreme Court might declare emancipation without compensation to be unconstitutional is, of itself, sufficient justification of the President's policy, corresponding to the above suggestions in this matter.

Such compensation will be unpopular with many. Wise and just acts, when they involve sacrifices, frequently are. A wrong long tolerated commonly entails a penalty, which is seldom cheerfully paid. Yet, even on other grounds, we ought not, in this case, to begrudge the money. Who deserve better of their country than those brave men who, in the border and other slave States, have clung to their loyalty through all the dark hours of peril even to life?

Precautions naturally suggest themselves against false pretences of loyalty. It seems expedient that he who shall have proved that he is the legal owner of certain slaves, and also that he has ever been loyal to the Union, should receive a certificate of indebtedness by the government, not transferable, to be paid at some fixed time subsequent to the termination of the war: payment being made contingent on the fact that the claimant shall not, meanwhile, have lapsed from his loyalty.

Every such claimant, once recognized, would feel himself to be, by his own act, the citizen of a free State; one of us, detached forever from the Southern league. A government stockholder, he would become pecuniarily interested in the support of the government and the restoration of peace.

The legislatures of the border States may not initiate such a policy, but the loyal men of these States will accept it.

Such a measure does not involve expense in conveying the liberated negro to other countries. It has hitherto, indeed, been the usual policy in slave States to discourage as dangerous, the residence there of free blacks; and hence an idea that colonization should be the concomitant of emancipation. Of *general* emancipation, there is no need whatever that it should be. Those who take up such an idea forget that the jealousy with which slave-holders regard the presence of free negroes springs out of the dread that these may infect with a desire for freedom the slaves around them, thus rendering them insubordinate. But when all are free there will be no slaves to incite, nor any chains to be broken by resort to insurrection.

It is no business of ours either to decide, for the liberated negro, where he shall dwell, or to furnish his traveling expenses. Freemen, black or white, should select their own dwelling-place and pay their own way.

As to the fears of competition in labor sought to be excited in the minds of the Northern workingman, they have foundation only in case emancipation be refused; for such refusal would flood the North with fugitives. If, on the contrary, emancipation be carried out, the strong local attachments of the negro will induce him, with rarest exceptions, to remain as a hired laborer where he worked as a slave. Thus humane masters will not lack sufficient working hands, of which colonization would deprive them. And if, notwithstanding the probable rise of Southern staples, profits, at first, should be less, the security of the planter will be greater. He will no longer lie down at night uncertain whether the morning's news may not be that his slaves have risen against him.

This is the paper view of the question. But all edicts, all proclamations, how wise and righteous soever, are but idle announcements now, if we lack courage and conduct to enforce them.

Courage we have. Raw levies have behaved like veterans. The skeletons of regiments, reduced to one-tenth their original number, attest the desperate valor with which they confronted death. Not with the rank and file is the blame! The leading! There has been the secret of failure.

With all the advantages of a just cause over our enemies, we have suffered them to outdo us in earnestness. We lack the enthusiasm which made irresistible the charge of Cromwell's Ironsides. We need the invincible impulse of a sentiment. We want, above all, leaders who know and feel what they are fighting for. This is a war in which mercenaries avail not. There must be a higher motive than the pay of a Swiss—a holier duty urging on, than the professional pride, or the blind obedience, of a soldier. By parliamentary usage a proposed measure is entrusted, for fostering care, to its friends. So should this war be. Its conduct should be confided to men whose hearts and souls are in it.

Again. It has long been one of our national sins that we pass by, with scarcely a rebuke, the gravest public offences. We utterly fail in holding to a strict accountability our public men. The result of such failure, in peace, had almost escaped our notice. In war we have now beheld its effects, flagrant and terrible.

It was not to be expected that among so many thousands of officers suddenly appointed there should not be some hundreds of incompetents. Such things must be. No one is to blame if, in field or garden, weeds spring up. The blame rests with him who leaves them there, to choke the crop and cumber the ground.

Accountability—that should be the watchward—ACCOUNTABILITY, stern, unrelenting! Office has its emoluments; let it have its responsibilities also. Let us *demand*, as Napoleon demanded, success from our leaders. The rub may work harshly War needs harsh rules. Actions are not to be measured in war by the standard of peace. The sentinel worn by extreme fatigue, who sleeps at his post, incurs the penalty of death. There is mercy in courts martial—drum-head courts-martial. A dozen officers shot, whenever the gravity of the offence demands it, may be the saving of life to tens of thousands of brave men.

Eighteen months have passed. Eight hundred millions have been spent. We have a million of armed men in the field. More than a hundred thousand rest in soldiers' graves And for all this what result? Is it strange if sometimes the heart sinks and resolution fails at the thought that from sheer administrative infirmity, the vast sacrifice may have been all in vain?

But let the Past go! Its fatal faults (difficult perhaps, to avoid, under an effort so sudden and so vast) can never be recalled. Doubtless they had their use. It needed the grievous incapacity we have witnessed, the stinging reverses we have suffered, the invasion even of free States we have lived to see commenced; it needed the hecatombs of dead piled up unavailingly on battle-field after battle-field—the desolate hearths, the broken-hearted survivors—it needed all this to pave the way for that emancipation which is the only harbinger of peace.

The Future! that is still ours to improve. Nor, if some clouds yet rest upon it, is it without bright promise. Signs of nascent activity, energy, and a resolution to hold accountable for the issue the leaders of our armies, are daily apparent. Better than all, the initiative in a true line of policy has been taken. The twenty-third of September has had its effect. The path of safety is before us; steep and rugged, indeed, but no longer doubtful nor obscure. A lamp has been lit to guide our steps; a lamp that may burn more brightly before a new year dawns upon us. The noble prayer of Ajax has been vouchsafed in our case. At last we have light to fight by.

We shall reach a quiet haven if we but follow faithfully and perseveringly that guiding light.

There is, at this moment, in the hearts of all good men throughout the length and breadth of the land, no deeper feeling, no more earnest longing, than for peace; peace not for the day, not to last for a few years; but peace on a foundation of rock, for ourselves and for our children after us. May the hearts of our rulers be opened to the conviction that they can purchase only a shambling counterfeit except at one cost! God give them to see, ere it be too late, that THE PRICE OF ENDURING PEACE IS GENERAL EMANCIPATION!

I am, sir, your obedient servant,

ROBERT DALE OWEN.

New York, November 10, 1862.

ιϋ Ag '12

www.ingramcontent.com/pod-product-compliance
Lightning Source LLC
Chambersburg PA
CBHW021555270326
41931CB00009B/1220